Photo : Baron

The
QUEEN ELIZABETH
 Coronation Souvenir

MCMLIII

The Duke of Edinburgh and his page.

The Earl Marshal waits to receive his Queen beneath the heraldic splendour of the Royal Arms as the State Coach approaches the Abbey.

The Queen, after her entry into the Abbey Church of Westminster, is seated in her Chair of Estate.

" God crown you with a crown of glory and righteousness."

Her Majesty the Queen

Mother with her pages.

Her Majesty the Queen with her Mistres

Robes and the six Maids of Honour.

The Archbishop of Canterbury, the Most Reverend Geoffrey Francis Fisher, D.D., stands before the Abbey Altar during the Coronation ceremony.

Before a sea of faces, the Sovereign's coach crosses Trafalgar Square.

The Queen, the Duke of Edinburgh and their children with other

members of the Royal Family on the balcony at Buckingham Palace.

Out of Hyde Park and under Marble Arch moves the great cavalcade.

The scarlet tunics of the Royal Canadian Mounted Police make a brave show as they ride through Piccadilly Circus.

A view from the Victoria Memorial as the State Coach approaches the Palace gates.

THE QUEEN IS CROWNED

by NEIL FERRIER

Looking back, on the evening of June the Second, over the events of Coronation day, the first thing one realises is that the Coronation has not just been a series of events, it has been a slowly developing state of mind and of feeling. Today has seen the culmination of the process, a deeply moving and symbolical religious ceremony, magnificent pomp and display; but the whole has been built up gradually. Perhaps that is why the weather today, and it has been mostly very bad weather, seems to have had curiously little effect on the proceedings.

Everyone has felt since the Queen came to the throne that in her the British Monarchy had found a very special kind of renewal. Young, beautiful, intelligent, charming; an exemplary wife and mother; God-fearing and of absolute integrity, she has appeared from the first moment of her reign—and indeed even before that—to be the ideal person for the task before her. In the tragic death of her father she had our sympathy, and in the courage and selflessness with which she immediately assumed the burdens of her new Queenly state she soon won our deepest respect. Our love she had no need to win — that was hers already.

As the months have passed leading up to the Coronation there has grown with increasing conviction an idea that the commonplaces which were uttered about the beginning of a " New Elizabethan Era " might really be true. As the street decorations went up and the pace of preparations rose to a crescendo people seemed to stir themselves, to look about with a new interest and a new hope, to believe once more that it was in their power to shape events and throw off the doubts and despondencies that oppressed them.

In all this, popular opinion looked to the Queen for inspiration and to her Coronation as a seal that should once and for all stamp this new charter of hope with authority.

And if people looked for an omen what better one could there have been than the news that greeted us all on the very morning of the Coronation, the news that a British expedition had finally conquered Everest. Once again a " Briton " (and it was the New Zealand Premier who, significantly, called his compatriot that) had been the first to do what no other had done, to stand where no other had stood. That was one side of the picture which cheered us as the day dawned, but there was another no less significant to be seen along the entire length of the Coronation route. There the people waited for their Queen, the temperature had fallen, worse still the rain had fallen—but their *spirits* had *not* fallen. They were not " grinning and bearing it "; they were simply ignoring it, denying that at such a time the state of the weather really mattered.

That was how the day, the Second of June, started and that was how it continued. The facts of it we all know, they are already a part of history, and like all history impersonal. But the quality of Coronation day that will make it linger in our minds is precisely that it was dominated by the personal and the individual element in it. What we remember is not a logical progress of events but a series of impressions.

First there was the departure of the great State Coach from Buckingham Palace. As it came through the Palace archway it looked immense, capable of dominating any background, almost unwieldy, and then turning out into the road it was suddenly dwarfed by the crowd and in the roar of their applause became quite fragile, a thing hardly real, moved apparently only by their enthusiasm, their conscious support.

To the children it was certainly that. As they

B

The Queen and the Duke of Edinburgh leaving Buckingham Palace in the great State Coach drawn by eight of the famous Windsor Greys. The Guard of Honour in front of the gates is formed by men of the Royal Navy, of the Irish Guards and of the Royal Air Force.

lined the Embankment what they saw was obviously pure magic. They cheered as perhaps no crowd has ever cheered before. *They* didn't mind about the rain. For those few minutes they probably did not know it *was* raining. They were seeing the coach, the uniforms, the horses; they were hearing dimly with the ear an Englishman always has for sounds from the sea, the noise of

sirens on the Thames—and they were seeing their Queen, someone young, radiant, as full of life as themselves.

Of course the strongest memories of the day concern the Abbey, for what went on there was the point and purpose of everything else. The Queen came there with her mind intent on assuming certain responsibilities and seeking, with

Her Majesty leaves the Palace wearing the exquisite gown designed by Mr. Norman Hartnell.   It is made of white satin and embroidered with the emblems of Great Britain and the Commonwealth.

The great day has really begun for the long-waiting crowds as the Queen's Procession goes down The Mall on its way to Westminster Abbey.

her people, God's aid in undertaking them.

Her air throughout the entire proceedings was one of resolve and the setting toned-in perfectly. Here was a building full of incidental graces but one in which clearly all detail was subordinate to a total effect of height, spaciousness, clarity. This was obviously a place for clear thought and serious action.

At the same time there was nothing oppressive or forbidding about the scene. All the bustle and colour of life had been crowded within these walls before the Queen arrived and, though quiet now, the whole scene was warm and alive, a rich feast to the eye. The peers and peeresses on opposite sides of the central theatre, the theatre itself with its wonderful golden carpet, the group of Bishops, the gleaming collection of plate on the altar, all these spoke of pomp and power and magnificence. Indeed these two notes sounded all through the service—a simplicity that was always noble, a magnificence that being devoted to high things was never ostentatious or falsely proud. Even in the furniture of the theatre, that aptly named raised central space on which the rites of coronation take place, there was this contrast, with the throne and its gorgeously worked royal cipher set off against the commanding plainness of the King Edward Chair.

Round these two chairs and the Chair of Estate there is to revolve a drama, a drama

All eyes are on the radiantly smiling young Queen as with the Duke of Edinburgh she drives in state to her Coronation.

moulded of contrast and high intent. But before the drama there is the prologue of the procession up the Nave of the Abbey. Here is the history that does not die, whether it be represented by the heralds in their beautiful quartered garments or show itself in the indomitable form of our own Prime Minister, the Right Honourable Sir Winston Churchill. Here is history alive in our day and touching to nobility both actor and watcher in their shared sense of being part of a larger unity outside time.

Yet from this massed display the mind travels to a very different picture. It contains only one figure, the Queen, and around her nothing *material* is happening. No-one moves or speaks,

and the solitary figure is on its knees in prayer. Curiously often we shall see this image of the lonely figure as the day passes, for solitude is the ordained burden of leaders and rulers. Others may help or advise them, but they alone are responsible.

As, after this moment of private prayer, the Queen moves on from stage to stage of her Coronation two Bishops move always at her sides to help her and they too seem to be conscious of this gulf that no willingness can cross. It is touching to watch their solicitude for the comfort of the Queen as they assist her to arrange her robes, to rise from or sit down in a chair, but it is more touching to see that the Queen is conscious

A closer view of Her Majesty leaving Buckingham Palace. The State Coach was built in the reign of George III, nearly two hundred years ago, and is now used only for Coronations.

A fine prospect of the Queen's Procession as it passes under Admiralty Arch and turns through Trafalgar Square into Northumberland Avenue.

Queen Elizabeth the Queen Mother and Princess Margaret ride in the Irish State Coach on their way to Westminster Abbey.

The Prime Minister of the United Kingdom, the Rt. Hon. Sir Winston Churchill, K.G., arrives at Westminster Abbey accompanied by Lady Churchill. Sir Winston wears the uniform of Lord Warden of the Cinque Ports.

Queen Elizabeth the Queen Mother leaves the Irish State Coach to enter Westminster Abbey beneath a magnificent representation of the Royal Arms, a notable feature of the Coronation annexe designed by Mr. Eric Bedford and other Ministry of Works architects.

The arrival at Westminster Abbey of Her Majesty the Queen accompanied by the Duke of Edinburgh. The standard of the Sovereign's Escort is lowered as she enters, while Guardsmen and men of the Royal Air Force present arms. In the crowd are many visitors from the Commonwealth and Colonies.

of their difficulty, that she seeks to reassure them from time to time by an extra decisiveness of carriage or movement as they hesitate that she is *not* overburdened, that their help is *not* insufficient.

The Archbishop of Canterbury has a presence that makes itself felt at once. When he speaks it is with calm authority that needs no embellishment to carry conviction. His question to the congregation, four times repeated to different quarters of the church during the Recognition, makes of this formal challenge a real one. When he asks of those who have come to do their homage and service " Are you willing to do the same ? " he is asking not for a bending of the knee but for a lifetime's devotion to the high standards of which the Queen is our pattern. Later in the Administration of the Oath he puts questions of similar weight to the Queen and here the response leaves us in no doubt. He asks of

the Queen whether she will govern the peoples set under her " according to their respective laws and customs ", if she will " cause Law and Justice in Mercy to be executed " and if she will maintain " the Laws of God " " the Protestant Reformed Religion" and "the Church of England". He is obviously not asking for mere lip service to these things and the Queen's replies are equally obviously as well-weighed as his questions when she says in a firm clear voice, " I solemnly promise so to do", " I will " and " all this I promise to do ".

To kiss the book, to sign the Oath are confirmations hardly needed after such avowals, but there seems a fitness in things when the Bible on which Queen Elizabeth has sworn her Oath is presented to her by the Archbishop of Canterbury and the Moderator of Scotland in conjunction. Her promises have been made for both countries, both countries look to the Bible for the inspiration of their national life, of both their national churches

The Queen alights from her coach with a gracious smile, assisted by her Maids of Honour and watched by the Duke of Edinburgh.

Inside the Abbey Church of St. Peter, the Royal Procession moves slowly down the Nave. The Queen's train is carried by her six Maids of Honour, followed by the Mistress of the Robes—the Dowager Duchess of Devonshire.

Her Majesty enters the Coronation Theatre and the Queen's Scholars of Westminster School greet her with their traditional cry of " Vivat ! Vivat ! Vivat Regina ! " On her right walks the Bishop of Durham ; on her left the Bishop of Bath and Wells.

the Queen is head. As so often in this service that has been polished to perfection through the centuries the words take precedence even of the people when, ending this little ceremony, the Moderator says " Here is wisdom ; This is the Royal Law ; These are the lively Oracles of God ".

The giving of gifts and the taking of vows strikes a familiar chord in the mind, the opening of the communion service establishes the pattern. The act of Coronation is in essence sacramental. As with the Communion Bread and Wine the gifts the Queen is now to receive stand for things beyond themselves. First is the gift of the Anointing. We see the Queen, helped from her magnificent robe, walk away leaving it held by the six maids of honour, as though she came without fetter of self-interest or pride to be dedicated to God. This is the unworldly gift of Grace, but those that follow, though they are in the material sense rich almost beyond price, each have an inner meaning as well. The Golden Spurs of knightly chivalry, the golden Armills or bracelets, newly presented by the Commonwealth and therefore doubly symbolic of unity between the Queen and God's purpose and between the Queen and her peoples, the jewelled Orb set under the Cross as " the whole world is subject to the Power and Empire of Christ our Redeemer ", all these are precious and meaningful. Meaningful too is the putting on of the Robe Royal of Cloth of Gold and the Stole, the giving of the Ring (sometimes appropriately called " the wedding ring of England ") and the presentation of the Sceptre and the Rod. Yet there persists in the memory one of the earlier presentations, that of the Jewelled Sword. It cannot be light, yet as the Queen sits holding it point upwards, it is as steady as in the hand of a fencing master. So it

The Queen passes through a brilliant company as she approaches her Chair of Estate. Behind the three Royal Dukes are many distinguished persons including the Earl of Halifax who wears the cloak of the Order of the Garter. In the foreground may be seen the Lord High Chancellor (Lord Simonds) and the Lord Great Chamberlain (the Marquess of Cholmondeley).

The Queen seated in her Chair of Estate. Members of the Royal Family stand in the gallery behind. On Her Majesty's right the Marquess of Salisbury bears the great Sword of State.

The Queen wearing a simple white garment awaits the sacred moment of the Anointing.

Seated now in the ancient King Edward's Chair—in which she is crowned—the Queen holds the jewelled sword which the Archbishop of Canterbury has brought to her from the altar.

stays through a long prayer. Then, rising, the Queen lowers the sword and holds it out before her at the altar as an offering. The strength and the submission are each appropriate to their moment and inherent in the woman who displays them.

The spectacular moment, the moment for which everyone in the Abbey is, in a sense, assembled, is the crowning. So many things impress it on the mind. The sense of physical and moral weight in the crown itself, displayed by the extra tension in the Archbishop and the Queen, the tremendous shouts of " God Save the Queen ", the mysteriously silent movement with which the Princes and Princesses, Peers and Peeresses assume their Coronets. This is the perfection of pure spectacle.

So is the Enthroning with the Queen being assisted by her Archbishops and Bishops, and the Homage with the Archbishop kneeling before her as representative of the kneeling Bishops.

Yet it is the personal touch we remember and the Duke of Edinburgh's words " I Philip, Duke of Edinburgh, do become your liege man of life and limb, and of earthly worship ; and faith and truth I will bear unto you, to live and die, against all manner of folks. So help me God ". We see him kiss her on the cheek, touch the Crown and step back. From then on it is the Queen we see, supporting the great weight of the Crown unflinchingly, as the senior peer of each order comes to pay fealty for his order.

After the Archbishop has enjoined her, " With this Sword do justice," the Queen rises and with memorable dignity replaces the Sword on the altar.

These are the magnificent moments and no-one who saw them will ever forget them. But perhaps the deepest impression the Coronation makes is when all its official acts are over. The Queen at this point has presented the Archbishop with the Bread and the Wine for the Communion and has given as oblations an altar cloth and an ingot of gold weighing a pound ; now she kneels down, all the insignia of Queenly power laid aside, and joins, in taking communion, with her husband, not as his sovereign but simply as the woman who is justly proud to be his wife.

The Archbishop places the Orb in the Queen's hands, saying : " Receive this Orb set under the Cross, and remember that the whole world is subject to the power and empire of Christ our Redeemer." The Queen afterwards hands the Orb to the Dean of Westminster who replaces it on the altar.

As the service ends we are conscious that many things half noticed in passing will linger in the mind when we have time to dwell on them. The orderliness and efficiency of all who played their part in the great mystery of the Coronation, the magnificence of the music in Parry's setting of the Psalm " I was glad when they said unto me, we will go into the house of the Lord ", the rousing glory of the fanfares, Handel's " Zadok the Priest " and Sir William Walton's powerful " Te Deum ".

But now the procession goes on its way and the memory fills with things seen briefly but memorably ; Queen Salote of Tonga refusing to

The climax of the great ceremony is at hand. The Queen has received in her right hand the Sceptre with the Cross, " the ensign of kingly power and justice " ; and in her left hand the Rod with the Dove. Now the Archbishop prepares to place St. Edward's Crown on her head.

have the hood of her carriage put up though the rain poured down on her unprotected head, the Prime Minister leaning half out of his carriage to wave in the Park, the gleam of bayonets along the beautifully decorated stretch of the Mall, the box-like formations neat and exact as toys rounding the Victoria Memorial outside Buckingham Palace.

Though the sky gloomed, and much of the time rain fell, the splendour of the great marching columns was not dimmed. Paradoxically it was brightened, for shining brass, scarlet coat, coloured cap or white topee stood out the more emphatically for having only greyness to compete with instead of the dazzle of sunshine. Amazingly, but not unexpectedly, the procession passed along its course without incident. Occasionally a restive

horse would carry a Life-Guardsman a pace or two in reverse, occasionally a few units might mark time or even halt for a few moments, but the total effect was one of practised ease as though it had all been done a thousand times before by everyone present and was the easiest thing in the world to do again.

A persistent memory and a nagging one is that of trying to spot the famous. Sometimes we found them ; all too often we failed. Yet in a sense we were satisfied to know them there, thinking of them not by their present titles but as they first impressed themselves on our memories— " Monty ", Field-Marshal Alexander, " Bomber " Harris.

Other memories are of how much pleasure the

St. Edward's Crown, which the Archbishop now places upon the Queen's head, is worn only at Coronations. It was made for King Charles II, but embodies portions of the more ancient crown which was destroyed at the time of the Commonwealth.

The Archbishop holds St. Edward's Crown aloft while throughout the Abbey the great assembly waits for the actual moment of Coronation.

Queen Elizabeth II is crowned ! A great cry goes up of " God Save The Queen ", and the Princes and Princesses, the Peers and Peeresses, put on their coronets. A fanfare of trumpets sounds throughout the Abbey, and at the Tower of London a salute of guns is fired.

A moment of solemn majesty as the Archbishop of Canterbury pronounces a benediction upon the newly crowned Queen.

An impressive view of the Abbey, looking towards the Nave, during the ceremony of the Homage. In the foreground stands the time-darkened King Edward's Chair, and resting beneath it is the famous Stone of Scone.

The Duke of Edinburgh does his Homage.   Kneeling before the Queen, he places his hands in hers and says : " I
truth I will bear unto you, to live and die,

Philip, Duke of Edinburgh, do become your liege man of life and limb, and of earthly worship; and faith and against all manner of folks. So help me God."

The Queen enthroned, attended by the Bishops of Durham and of Bath and Wells. Immediately behind Her Majesty stands Marshal of the Royal Air Force the Viscount Portal of Hungerford, holding the Sceptre with the Cross.

After the Duke of Edinburgh has spoken the words of the Homage he rises, touches the Crown, and then kisses the Queen on the left cheek.

Prince Charles, seated in the Royal Box between Queen Elizabeth the Queen Mother and Princess Margaret, is plainly fascinated by all that is going on. He was brought into the Abbey by a side door in time to witness the actual ceremony of his mother's crowning.

Royal Family give ; Queen Elizabeth the Queen Mother with her gracious inclination of the head and heart warming smile (a gallant defiance of memories that must often have intruded), the Queen bearing her Orb and Sceptre, acknowledging the deafening cheering that accompanied her along the route.

The memorable day draws towards its close ; the State Coach passes from sight and the processions disperse, but outside the Palace the crowd swells and the Royal Family appear to watch the fly past of the Royal Air Force. The Air Force certainly make a very impressive noise, but there are so many aeroplanes and only one Prince Charles. Perhaps we may be forgiven for remembering his imitation of his mother's wave when we have forgotten how many types of aircraft were represented.

Most British festivities begin or end in the home. The Queen's day had done both, and many of her subjects following her example were beside their own firesides at 9 o'clock when she made her broadcast. The words that she spoke are contained elsewhere in this book. What cannot be reproduced is the conviction with which she spoke them ; the immediacy with which she was present to us. For those who heard her this surely is the right memory on which to take leave of Coronation day, the day on which in the fine words of the Bishop of Exeter " this modest, unassuming, gentle woman and mother, representing neither talent nor party nor programme nor interest nor class, but possessing all the qualities that are lovely in private life " became " by acclamation ' with one voice and consent of tongue and heart ' the highest in the land."

Side by side, the Queen and the Duke of Edinburgh kneel before the Abbey altar during the Communion Service which follows the Crowning and Homage.

A scene of the greatest brilliance is unfolded as the Queen slowly returns up the Nave at the conclusion of the service She has now exchanged the heavy St. Edward's Crown for the jewel-encrusted Imperial State Crown, made for Queen Victoria in 1838.

Wearing her Imperial State Crown, carrying both Orb and Sceptre, the crowned Queen leaves the Abbey to receive the renewed acclamation of her peoples.

HER MAJESTY'S CORONATION BROADCAST

The Queen in her broadcast to the world said :
" When I spoke to you last, at Christmas, I asked you all, whatever your religion, to pray for me on the day of my Coronation—to pray that God would give me wisdom and strength to carry out the promises that I should then be making.

Throughout this memorable day I have been uplifted and sustained by the knowledge that your thoughts and prayers were with me.

I have been aware all the time that my peoples, spread far and wide throughout every continent and ocean in the world, were united to support me in the task to which I have now been dedicated with such solemnity.

Many thousands of you came to London from all parts of the Commonwealth and Empire to join in the ceremony, but I have been conscious too of the millions of others who have shared in it by means of wireless or television in their homes.

All of you, near or far, have been united in one purpose.

It is hard for me to find words in which to tell you of the strength which this knowledge has given me.

The ceremonies you have seen to-day are ancient, and some of their origins are veiled in the mists of the past. But their spirit and their meaning shine through the ages—never, perhaps, more brightly than now. I have in sincerity pledged myself to your service, as so many of you are pledged to mine. Throughout all my life and with all my heart I shall strive to be worthy of your trust.

In this resolve I have my husband to support me. He shares all my ideals and all my affection for you. Then, although my experience is so short and my task so new, I have in my parents and grandparents an example which I can follow with certainty and with confidence.

There is also this. I have behind me not only the splendid traditions and the annals of more than a thousand years but the living strength and majesty of the Commonwealth and Empire : of societies old and new, of lands and races different in history and origins, but all, by God's will, united in spirit and in aim.

Therefore I am sure that this, my Coronation, is not the symbol of a power and a splendour that are gone but a declaration of our hopes for the future, and for the years I may, by God's grace and mercy, be given to reign and serve you as your Queen.

I have been speaking of the vast regions and varied peoples to whom I owe my duty, but there has also sprung from our island home a theme of social and political thought which constitutes our message to the world and through the changing generations has found acceptance both within and far beyond my realms.

Parliamentary institutions, with their free speech and respect for the rights of minorities, and the inspiration of a broad tolerance in thought and its expression—all this we conceive to be a precious part of our way of life and outlook.

During recent centuries, this message has been sustained and invigorated by the immense contribution, in language, literature, and action, of the nations of our Commonwealth overseas.

It gives expression, as I pray it always will, to living principles as sacred to the Crown and Monarchy as to its many parliaments and peoples.

I ask you now to cherish them, and practise them too : then we can go forward together in peace, seeking justice and freedom for all men.

As this day draws to its close, I know that my abiding memory of it will be not only the solemnity and beauty of the ceremony but the inspiration of your loyalty and affection.

I thank you all from a full heart. God bless you all."

THE HAPPIEST SMILE OF THE YEAR
The Queen waves to the cheering crowds as she drives to the House of Lords for the State Opening of Parliament,
November, 1952.

D

Caroline Hunt, daughter of the Director of the Old Vic, presents a posy to Her Majesty the Queen, before the Gala Performance of *King Henry VIII* on the 6th May.

This photograph is one of a number of especially pleasing studies taken in the grounds of Balmoral. Here the Queen, with her two children, is watching the antics of her dogs. Several of these photographs were released for publication to mark the occasion of Prince Charles' fourth birthday.

A charming study of Prince Charles and Princess Anne taken by Marcus Adams also for the occasion of Prince Charles' fourth birthday.

AT BALMORAL

Prince Charles halts his make-believe horse to give the photographer this happy picture.

Photos : Studio Lisa

Princess Anne was not far away. Not to be outdone, she is using the other arm of the garden seat as the back of a horse.

The Queen, who was accompanied by the Duke of Edinburgh and Princess Margaret, celebrated her wedding anniversary, 20th November, 1952, at the Coliseum, where she saw the musical show *Call Me Madam*.

Her Majesty arriving at the Festival Hall, London, to attend the Royal Concert in aid of the Musician's Benevolent Fund and other charities. 24th November, 1952.

The Queen with Prince Charles and Princess Anne returned to London in February from her holiday at Sandringham.

A study by Marcus Adams of Prince Charles and Princess Anne.

One of a series of photographs taken by Baron just before the Coronation.   Her Majesty wears the Star and Ribbon of the Order of the Garter.

Her Majesty meets a famous predecessor. At a gala performance of *King Henry VIII* she is shown chatting to Paul Rogers, who took the name part in the play.

The Queen gave the first big party of her reign in December 1952 when she entertained the Prime Ministers of the Commonwealth to dinner at Buckingham Palace. She is shown here with Mr. S. G. Holland (New Zealand), Sir Winston Churchill, Mr. Robert Menzies (Australia) and Mr. St. Laurent (Canada).

The Olympic Horse Trials were held at Badminton in April.   Her Majesty the Queen and the Duke of Edinburgh were present and our photograph shows them watching the Trials from a vantage point in a LandRover car.

The country responded overwhelmingly to the Lord Mayor of London's Fund for the relief of flood distress. In the photograph the Queen and the Duke of Edinburgh are shown arriving at the Albert Hall to attend a special concert in aid of the Fund, given by the London Philharmonic Orchestra.

Princess Anne is a rewarding subject for the photographer's art.   This photograph is one taken by Marcus Adams.

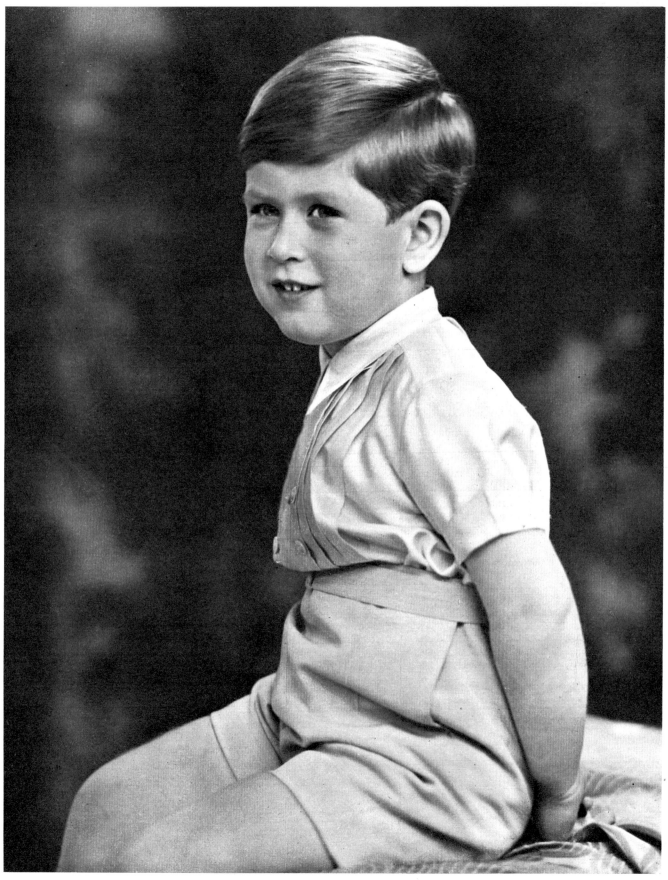

His Royal Highness Prince Charles was four years old on the 14th November, 1952. Here is a photograph taken for the occasion by Marcus Adams.

Another of the pleasing group of photographs taken by Studio Lisa at Balmoral.   Her Majesty is shown relaxing
in the lovely surroundings of her Scottish home.

On the same occasion the photographer obtained this study of Princess Anne with her doll and pram happily showing how well she could manage the complicated business of raising the hood.

E

While in Clydeside for the launching of the new Royal yacht *Britannia*, Her Majesty paid a visit to Dumbarton. Here she is shown receiving the keys of the Castle.

The Queen with Princess Margaret leaving the Coliseum Theatre, London, after a performance of *Call Me Madam*. The occasion celebrated the anniversary of the Royal wedding on 20th November.

One of the most splendid and colourful occasions preceding the Coronation was the presentation of new standards to the Household Cavalry. The ceremony took place at Windsor. Here Prince Charles arrives with his aunt, Princess Margaret.

Her Majesty in happy mood stands upon the dais from which she reviewed the parade of the Household Cavalry.

Her Majesty presenting one of the standards to the Life Guards.

After the standards were presented and paraded, it pleased the spectators and the viewers on television to see Prince Charles rejoin his mother. He had been watching her during the whole of the ceremony. Here the Queen is about to assist the young Prince into the car.

One of the most effective photographs of the year is this picture taken at Home Park, Windsor, whil
dais to the right of the picture to take the salute as her royal standard floats above her.   The grey
fitting background for a military ceremony displaying all the colour an

the standards newly presented by Her Majesty the Queen were being paraded. She stands on the mass of Windsor Castle and the green trees which cover the slope beneath its walls provide a precision which is so much the tradition of the Household troops.

Her Majesty the Queen talking to the Duke of Edinburgh before the curtain rose for the Gala Performance of *King Henry VIII* on the 6th of May. She carries the posy presented to her by the daughter of the Director of the Old Vic.

The contending teams in the 1953 Cup Final were presented to the Duke of Edinburgh before the kick-off. Here His Royal Highness is shaking hands with Stanley Matthews, of Blackpool, who is possibly the most famous player today.

Watched by some of the many people who were daily arriving in London to witness the Coronation, the Queen and the Queen Mother arrive for the coming-out party of Miss Elizabeth Ward on the 20th May.

During the week preceding the Coronation, the Duke of Edinburgh made a number of visits to the troops newly arrived in this country for the occasion. Several times he made practical use of air transport, travelling by helicopter from the grounds of Buckingham Palace. Here he is entering the aircraft which landed him on the barrack square at Woolwich ten minutes later.

The whole nation followed with interest the progress of the Duke of Edinburgh's flying training.   Here he is
seen about to take the controls of a plane which bears the insignia of his rank.

The Duke of Edinburgh opened an exhibition of Royal yachts at the National Maritime Museum, Greenwich, in May. This photograph shows him on that occasion wearing the uniform of Admiral of the Fleet and bearing upon his left sleeve the wings which he had recently won.

As Coronation day approached, the rehearsals at the Abbey became more and more frequent. Commencing with particular parts and leading up to the complete ceremony. The picture shows Her Majesty the Queen and the Duke of Edinburgh arriving at Westminster Abbey for a rehearsal which included the actual Crowning ceremony.

The representatives of Parliaments and Legislatures, Members of the Commonwealth Parliamentary Association, took luncheon with Her Majesty the Queen in historic Westminster Hall on 27th May. The photograph shows the Queen delivering her speech from the high table.

Queen Elizabeth the Queen Mother—a radiant figure on the day of her daughter's coronation.

Princess Margaret—a fairy tale Princess in her dress of pure white satin embroidered with silver diamante and pearls.

Rain and cloud can do nothing to damp the enthusiasm of the crowds who cheer the Queen and the Duke of Edinburgh as they ride along Piccadilly in the State Coach flanked by Royal servants and Yeomen of the Guard.

The State Coach passes under the archway at Hyde Park Corner and enters the East Carriage Road. On the right Apsley House, the home of the great Duke of Wellington, is practically hidden by the stands erected round it.

Along Cockspur Street, across Trafalgar Square and under Admiralty Arch the great procession makes its way. Many spectators here were able to see it pass no less than three times.

Here come the Mounties! There is a warm welcome for these detachments from the Royal Canadian Mounted Police, in their scarlet tunics, as they turn from Whitehall into Trafalgar Square.

The jewels glistening in the Imperial State Crown are no brighter than the Queen's smile as she acknowledges the cheers which accompany her progress from end to end of the processional route.

From the four corners of the earth they came. Commonwealth and Colonial troops marching along the East Carriage Road towards Marble Arch.

A great favourite with the crowds is Queen Salote of Tonga who, accompanied by the Sultan of Kelantan, ignores the frequently heavy rain and continues to ride in an open carriage, followed by an escort of Mounted Military Police.

Framed in a delicate tracery of a triumphal arch, the State Coach moves along London's great processional way, The Mall. In the foreground a Guards band strikes up the National Anthem as the Queen passes.

Men of the Royal Navy present arms as the royal couple near the end of their five mile progress from Westminster Abbey to Buckingham Palace.

The moment for which everyone has been waiting. The Royal Family appear on the balcony of Bucking
those present (reading from left to right) are the Duchess of Gloucester, the Princess Royal, Her Majesty's six M
Elizabeth the Queen Mother, Princess Margaret, Prince Richard, Prince William, Princess Marie Louise,

...ace to acknowledge the cheers of the densely packed crowds and to watch the fly-past of the R.A.F. Among ...Honour, The Queen, Prince Charles, Princess Anne, the Duke of Edinburgh, the Duke of Gloucester, Queen ...chess of Kent, Prince Michael, Princess Alexandra, the Duke of Kent, and Princess Alice Countess of Athlone.

A happy moment on the Palace balcony.   The Queen and the Duke exchange smiles while Prince Charles and Princess Anne are absorbed with the planes roaring overhead.

Down below the crowds have broken through the cordons and surge right up to the Palace gates through which, only a few hours before, the Queen set forth to her Coronation.

Waving and smiling, the Queen and the Duke of Edinburgh take a last look at the cheering crowds before following the other members of the Royal Family back into the Palace.

In London it is a night of celebrations which reach their climax in the gigantic firework display on the South Bank. Here is one of its biggest moments : a set-piece portraying the Queen, the Duke of Edinburgh and their two children.

Another brilliant burst of colour lights up the Thames throwing the old Shot Tower on South Bank into sharp relief. In the foreground Waterloo Bridge is garlanded with lights, while in the distance can be seen both Big Ben and the floodlit towers of the Abbey.

Her Majesty Queen Elizabeth II, crowned and wearing her robes, with His Royal Highness the Duke of Edinburgh. This photograph was taken at Buckingham Palace shortly after their return from Westminster Abbey.

The Queen with her Mistress of the Robes (the Dowager Duchess of Devonshire) and the six Maids of Honour who attended the Queen and carried her Majesty's train in Westminster Abbey.

A Coronation Day group taken at the Palace which shows the Queen and other members of the Royal Family together with some of the foreign dignitaries who attended.

A real family group at the Palace which includes (looking from left to right) Prince Michael, the Duke of Kent, the Duchess of Kent, Crown Princess Marthe of Norway, Crown Prince Olaf of Norway, Princess Margaret, the Queen, the Duke of Edinburgh, Prince Charles, Princess Anne, Queen Elizabeth the Queen Mother, the Earl of Athlone, the Duke of Gloucester, the Princess Royal, the Earl of Harewood, Prince Richard, the Duchess of Gloucester, Prince William, and Princess Alice Countess of Athlone.

The Crowned Queen, holding Orb and Sceptre, rides through London in her Golden Coach.

MADE AND PRINTED IN GREAT BRITAIN BY L. T. A. ROBINSON LTD., LONDON, S.W.9.

Photo : Baron